S0-BBF-348

Pioneers to the West

John Bliss

Raintree

Chicago, Illinois

SOUTH HUNTINGTON
PUBLIC LIBRARY
HUNTINGTON STA.,NY
11746

www.heinemannraintree.com
Visit our website to find out more information about Heinemann-Raintree books.

To order:
☎ Phone 888-454-2279
💻 Visit www.heinemannraintree.com to browse our catalog and order online.

© 2012 Raintree
an imprint of Capstone Global Library, LLC
Chicago, Illinois

Visit our website at www.heinemannraintree.com

All rights reserved. No part of this publication may be reproduced or transmitted in any form or by any means, electronic or mechanical, including photocopying, recording, taping, or any information storage and retrieval system, without permission in writing from the publisher.

Edited by Louise Galpine, Abby Colich, and Diyan Leake
Designed by Richard Parker
Original illustrations © Capstone Global Library Ltd 2011
Illustrated by Jeff Edwards
Picture research by Mica Brancic
Originated by Capstone Global Library Ltd
Printed and bound in the United States of America, North Mankato, MN

15 14 13 12 11
10 9 8 7 6 5 4 3 2

Library of Congress Cataloging-in-Publication Data
Bliss, John, 1958-
  Pioneers to the West / John Bliss.
    p. cm.—(Children's true stories. Migration)
  Includes bibliographical references and index.
  ISBN 978-1-4109-4076-6 (hc)—ISBN 978-1-4109-4082-7
(pb) 1. Pioneers—West (U.S.)—History—Juvenile literature.
2. Frontier and pioneer life—West (U.S.)—Juvenile literature.
3. West (U.S.)—History—19th century—Juvenile literature. I.
Title.
  F596.B54 2012
  978'.02—dc22   2010039341

Acknowledgments
The author and publishers are grateful to the following for permission to reproduce copyright material: Bridgeman Art Library p. **7** (Private Collection/Peter Newark American Pictures); Corbis p. **10** (© Bettmann); © Corbis p. **26** (Bettmann); Getty Images pp. **4** (MPI), **8** (SuperStock/ Jerome Kleine), **9** (Hulton Archive/Henry Guttmann), **12** (MPI), **18** (Time Life Pictures/Pix Inc./Nina Leen), **22** (Historic Photo Archive); Library of Congress pp. **16**, **20** (Rare Book and Special Collections Division); Little House on the Prairie Museum, Independence, Kansas p. **15**; Courtesy of the National Orphan Train Complex, Concordia, Kansas p. **23** (Anna Laura Hill Collection); Nebraska State Historical Society p. **25** (Library/Archives); Rex Features p. **19** (NBCUPhotobanks); Scala Florence p. **13** (Digital Image 2010 © Smithsonian American Art Museum/Art Resource New York); State Archives of the South Dakota State Historical Society, Pierre, SD 57501 p. **14**; Woolaroc Museum, Oklahoma, USA p. **27**.

Cover photograph of a family assembled in front of a log cabin, Utah, 1875, reproduced with the permission of Corbis (© Bettmann).

We would like to acknowledge the following sources of material: p. **5** from the American Poems website. http://www.americanpoems.com/poets/waltwhitman/13290. Accessed on November 22, 2010; pp. **7–9** from "Surviving the Westward Trek," by Maurine Jensen Proctor and Scot Facer Proctor, *Meridian Magazine*, 2006. http://www.ldsmag.com/books/060723surviving.html. Accessed on October 6, 2010; p. **11** from "Children and Young People on the Overland Trail," Ruth Barnes Moynihan, *The Western Historical Quarterly*, Vol. 6, No. 3 (Jul., 1975), pp. 279–94; p. **12** from *Pioneer Children on the Journey West* by Emmy Werner, Boulder: Westview Press, 1995, p. 1. Found online at http://www.jstor.org/stable/967592. Accessed on October 6, 2010; p. **24** from the Nebraska Studies wesbite, http://www.nebraskastudies.org/0500/stories/0501_0210_01.html. Accessed on November 22, 2010.

We would like to thank Professor Sarah Chinn for her invaluable help in the preparation of this book.

Every effort has been made to contact copyright holders of any material reproduced in this book. Any omissions will be rectified in subsequent printings if notice is given to the publisher.

Disclaimer
All the Internet addresses (URLs) given in this book were valid at the time of going to press. However, due to the dynamic nature of the Internet, some addresses may have changed, or sites may have changed or ceased to exist since publication. While the author and publisher regret any inconvenience this may cause readers, no responsibility for any such changes can be accepted by either the author or the publisher.

082011
006318RP

Contents

DAILY LIFE

Read here to learn what life was like for the children in these stories, and the impact that migrating had at home and at school.

NUMBER CRUNCHING

Find out the details about migration and the numbers of people involved.

Migrants' Lives

Read these boxes to find out what happened to the children in this book when they grew up.

HELPING HAND

Find out how people and organizations have helped children to migrate.

On the Scene

Read eyewitness accounts of migration in the migrants' own words.

Some words are printed in bold, **like this**. You can find out what they mean by looking in the glossary.

Westward Ho!

In the 1800s, Americans started moving west. These settlers, or **pioneers**, left their homes for many reasons. Some were looking for new farmland. Others went in search of gold. Some were drawn by adventure or by the chance to start new businesses. For all of them, the trip west meant a new life.

People often joined together on their journeys west. The lucky ones rode in covered wagons. Others walked many miles every day.

Whose land?

As these settlers headed west, they sometimes came into conflict with American Indians. The U.S. government had taken Indian lands for the pioneers to settle. Some Indians refused to leave without a fight.

Many children traveled with their families to the west. Some even went on their own. About 1 out of every 5 pioneers was younger than 18 years old. Between 1840 and 1865, about 40,000 children went west. This book will explore the stories of some of these young pioneers.

On the Scene

In 1855 U.S. poet Walt Whitman published his poem "Pioneers! O Pioneers!" In these lines from the poem, he describes the people heading west:

> O you youths, Western youths,
> So impatient, full of action, full of manly pride and friendship,
> Plain I see you Western youths, see you tramping with the
> foremost,
> Pioneers! O pioneers!

What kind of person do these words make you think about?

Western Illinois: 1848

Mormons believe in a type of Christianity that developed in the United States in the 1830s. They first settled in western Illinois, but conflicts with their neighbors made them head west. In 1846 they followed their leader, Brigham Young, to the Salt Lake Valley. Today, this is in the state of Utah. But in 1846, it was not yet part of the United States.

The Mormon Trail was the path Mormons followed from Illinois to present-day Utah. It stretched about 2,100 kilometers (1,300 miles), from the Mississippi River to the Salt Lake Valley.

George Staples

George Staples was born in England. As the oldest son in his family, he went to the United States to seek his fortune. Meanwhile, his parents raised the money for the rest of the family to follow. In 1848 George headed west from Illinois with a group of Mormon pioneers. He was only 14 years old.

George grew sick on the road. His fellow travelers did not want to stop and wait for George to recover. So, they left him with a local fur trapper.

Between 1846 and 1869, about 70,000 people followed the Mormon Trail.

HELPING HAND

The trapper whom George stayed with was friendly with a tribe of American Indians called the **Sioux**. Using **herbal** cures from local plants, a Sioux woman nursed George back to health.

Life among the Sioux

George soon grew well. He wanted to return to his people, but the Sioux could not understand his language. They cared for George and treated him as one of their own. As time passed, George began to enjoy his new life. He dressed in Sioux clothing and followed the Sioux's ways.

In the mid-1800s, American Indians made their clothing from plants and animal skins. They sometimes used feathers and shells for decoration.

DAILY LIFE

In the mid-1850s, young American Indian boys played with toy bows and arrows and rode fake horses. They also played a game called "shinny," which was like hockey. Players used wooden sticks to push a ball into a goal.

The lost boy found

By 1850 George's father, James, had arrived in Salt Lake. He heard stories from travelers who had seen a white boy living with the Sioux. Finally, a group of settlers went looking for George. When the young boy saw his father, he ran into his arms.

American Indian life seemed strange to the new settlers.

George never forgot his Sioux mother, and he visited her often. As a man, he wrote **treaties** (agreements) between the Mormons and the local Indian tribes.

9

Central Illinois: 1849

In 1848 an inspector visited a **sawmill** in California. A sawmill is a building where logs are cut into boards. In a ditch, the inspector noticed something glittering in the water. It turned out to be gold.

Many people were inspired to travel west by posters like this.

On the Scene

Helping people travel to California was big business during the Gold Rush. Many businessmen made more money by organizing trips to California than miners made by finding gold.

At first, the sawmill's owner, John Sutter, was able to keep the discovery secret. But word got out, and soon thousands of people were flocking to California. The Gold Rush was on! People who went to California in search of gold became known as **Forty-Niners**. They got this name because the Gold Rush began in 1849.

Miners set up camps wherever they found gold. The trail of camps became known as the "Golden Chain." If there was enough gold, a mining camp could grow into a town. Some of these towns still survive today.

Bound for California

John McWilliams, of Griggsville, Illinois, was not a typical Forty-Niner. He was often sick as a boy, and his mother and brother had both died of lung disease. But by 1849, when he was 16, John told his father he was "going to California, or die."

John set out with three friends from home. Unlike many pioneers, he was never sick on the trail.

11

In California

John did not have much luck when it came to mining. He and his friends did not know much about finding gold. He wrote, "The California gold diggings of which we thought so much, didn't look like a bit as we thought they would. In my imagination I thought I was going to dig gold out by the bucket-full."

rocker box

Early miners used "rocker boxes" to separate gold from other rocks in a river.

Then, one day, John met a friend from home. He showed John how to use mining tools. John was a quick learner, and he found $100 worth of gold in one day.

John McWilliams

John's luck did not hold. By the spring of 1850, he and his friends decided to move on. John's adventures then took him to Panama (in Central America) and New Orleans, Louisiana. He finally settled in St. Louis, Missouri, and raised a family. His granddaughter became the famous chef Julia Child.

This painting by artist Charles Christian Nahl is called "Miners in the Sierra." Nahl painted it in 1851.

HELPING HAND

A man named Levi Strauss made his fortune by inventing something the miners needed. He made a new kind of pants that could withstand the tough life of the miners. The jeans that many people wear today were invented by Levi Strauss.

Wisconsin: 1870

Not all of the pioneers were living with American Indians or searching for gold. Most lived simple lives, working on farms or raising animals. Some moved many times, always looking for the next **opportunity**, or chance to make their lives better.

Laura Ingalls is shown here with her parents and her three sisters, Mary, Carrie, and Grace. Laura is the middle girl in the back row.

Laura Ingalls

Laura got a love of reading and learning from her mother. From her father, she got a combination of independence and adventure. Charles Ingalls called himself a "Pioneer Man." Laura would later call herself a "Pioneer Girl."

To the prairie

Laura Ingalls was born in 1867 in Wisconsin. She was the second of four girls in her family. She also had a little brother, but he died before he was a year old. It was not unusual for children to die young in those days.

When Laura was only three years old, the family moved to Kansas. Laura's father had heard there was good farmland in Kansas. At the time, this was still Indian **Territory**. American Indians lived there and laid claim to it.

Laura called her Kansas home the "Little House on the **Prairie**." (Prairie is land made up of open fields of grass.) This picture shows what it would have looked like inside.

Many journeys

After a year in Kansas, money problems forced the Ingalls family back to Wisconsin. Laura's father, Charles, was always looking for new opportunities, and soon the family moved to Minnesota. There they lived in a **dugout** house. This was a house that was actually "dug out" of the earth. They had a dirt floor and grass on the roof.

The Ingalls family would have lived in a dugout house like this one. Dugout houses were small and hard to keep clean. But they were warm in winter and cool in summer.

DAILY LIFE

Most settlers had a stove that they used for both heat and cooking. They burned whatever fuel they could find. If they did not have wood, they burned hay, or even "chips." These were dried cow droppings.

Dakota Territory

When Laura was 12 years old, the family moved for the last time. Charles settled his family in the Dakota Territory, in what is now De Smet, South Dakota.

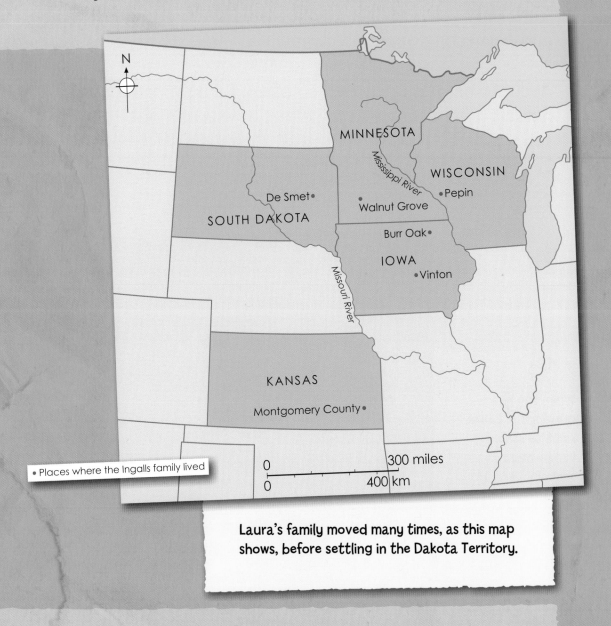

• Places where the Ingalls family lived

300 miles
400 km

Laura's family moved many times, as this map shows, before settling in the Dakota Territory.

Life in Dakota was hard. The winter of 1880 was very cold and snowy. The many **blizzards**, or snowstorms, cut off all supplies. The family struggled to survive.

School days

Most pioneer children went to school only when they could. Other tasks, such as helping out at home, often came first. The school year usually ran from October to May. That way, children could be at home for planting and harvesting on family farms.

Because her family moved so often, Laura mostly taught herself. When she went to school, it was in a one-room schoolhouse. There, children of all ages learned together. Laura and her sisters sometimes walked several miles to school.

When she was growing up, Laura went to school in one-room schoolhouses, like this one.

During her time in the Dakotas, Laura met a farmer named Almanzo Wilder. They married in 1885. Laura was then called Laura Ingalls Wilder, the name people know her as today through her well-known books (see box).

Laura Ingalls Wilder

Many years later, when she was in her sixties, Laura started writing about her experiences as a girl. In all, she wrote eight books about life on the **frontier** (unexplored land). These "Little House" books are still favorites of readers today.

This is a scene from the popular television series made in the 1970s, which was based on Laura Ingalls Wilder's books.

19

Missouri: 1883

If someone offered you land for free, would you take it? This is just what the U.S. government did when it passed the **Homestead** Act of 1862. A homestead was a piece of land a person could own simply by living on it for five years. The government had taken this land from American Indians.

Many people took the government's offer. Families moved west with their children to start a new life.

Advertisements like this helped create excitement for the Homestead Act. Even when the land was not free, the price for it was very low.

Ruth Chrisman

Ruth Chrisman headed west from Missouri with her family in 1883, when she was 11 years old. Her father raised cattle, which he sent west by train. The family—Ruth, her parents, her three sisters, and her three brothers—followed in wagons. Along with the family, those five wagons carried everything they owned.

After meeting the train, they traveled another 137 kilometers (85 miles) to their homestead, which was 23 kilometers (14 miles) north of Broken Bow, Nebraska.

Ruth was born in Waverly, Missouri. Her family moved to Broken Bow, in the Nebraska Territory. You can follow their journey on this map.

NUMBER CRUNCHING

Between 1860 and 1870, the population of Nebraska grew from 29,000 to 123,000. That is almost 100,000 new people in just 10 years!

Life on the prairie

Soon the Chrisman family had settled in Nebraska. Ruth—called Babe by her family—helped with the work. She gathered wild fruit, such as plums and raspberries, in the nearby canyon. She loved the long summer days, when the prairie grass was taller than she was.

Many pioneers like Ruth's family lived in houses made of **sod**, which is just dirt held together by grass.

Winters were hard on the open **range**, meaning the areas of open grassland where cattle were raised. Storms swept across the prairie, and cattle—and sometimes people—would get lost and freeze to death. When she was 17 years old, Ruth started teaching school. She was in the classroom when a blizzard struck. She saved the lives of her students by taking them to a nearby house until the storm passed. It took three days.

Between 1854 and 1929, more than 100,000 children went west on "orphan trains" (see panel below).

HELPING HAND

Some children went west without their parents. Poor and homeless children were sent on trains west from New York to live with farm families. The Children's Aid Society, which organized these "orphan trains," still serves needy children today. Though many of these children were treated well, some were forced to work very hard.

New homesteaders

Both men and women could own a homestead. A person just had to be 21 years old. So, as each of the Chrisman sisters turned 21, she claimed her own land. First came Lizzie, followed by Lutie Belle, and then Hattie. Unfortunately, by the time Ruth was 21, all of the best land had already been claimed.

On the Scene

Families on the prairie had to make their own fun. Ruth remembered the following stories about her prairie childhood:

[Since] our neighbors were such a long distance when we visited each other we spent several days. . . . How happy we were when we would look out and see someone coming over the hill. . . . [We] knew they were coming for the Nite: [we] only had three rooms in our sod house—but always had room for all that came. . . . We would take down a bed or two—put the table out side and be ready for a dance. My Brother played the violin so we had our orchestra at home—[we] often danced till daylight.

This photograph of the Chrisman sisters was taken in 1886. From left to right are Hattie, Lizzie, Lutie Belle, and Ruth. Ruth never liked the way she looked in this picture.

From Sea to Shining Sea

In 1845 a U.S. magazine writer said it was his country's "Manifest **Destiny**," or fate, to stretch from the Atlantic Ocean to the Pacific Ocean. By the end of the 1800s, that dream came true, as western lands were settled and turned into new U.S. states.

NUMBER CRUNCHING

From 1850 to 1896, 15 new states joined the United States. The nation more than doubled in size.

This painting by artist John Gast is called *American Progress*. It was painted in 1872. The country is shown as a woman moving from the cities on the east coast, past the Mississippi River, and heading toward the west coast.

But this destiny came at a price. Throughout the 1800s, thousands of American Indians were forced off the land that their people had lived on for hundreds of years. They were sent to live in special places set up by the government, called **reservations**. Those who refused to leave faced the force of the U.S. Army. This is a sad chapter in U.S. history.

Starting in 1838, the U.S. government sent thousands of American Indians from their homelands in the east to Oklahoma. This journey became know as the "Trail of Tears."

Building a new country

As the stories in this book have shown, life was hard for U.S. pioneer children. They had to work as hard as the adults. Many died young. But those who lived could be proud that they had helped build a country.

Mapping migration

Most settlers followed one of these trails to the west. Traveling a well-known path made the trip safer. This map also shows the route American Indians in the east followed to reservations in the west. This path was called the "Trail of Tears."

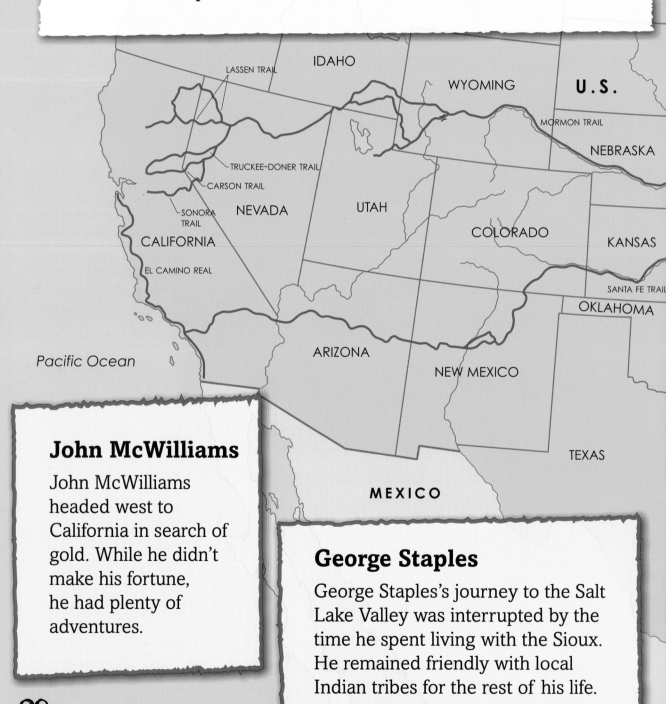

John McWilliams

John McWilliams headed west to California in search of gold. While he didn't make his fortune, he had plenty of adventures.

George Staples

George Staples's journey to the Salt Lake Valley was interrupted by the time he spent living with the Sioux. He remained friendly with local Indian tribes for the rest of his life.

N

CANADA

Laura Ingalls Wilder

The Ingalls family lived in many different places throughout the Midwest. As an adult, Laura Ingalls Wilder wrote about their experiences in books that are still popular today.

COUNCIL BLUFFS ROAD

IOWA

ILLINOIS

Missouri R.

MISSOURI

KENTUCKY

TRAIL OF TEARS (LAND ROUTE)

TENNESSEE R.

Mississippi R.

ARKANSAS

Tennessee R.

TRAIL OF TEARS (WATER ROUTE)

Atlantic Ocean

MISSISSIPPI

ALABAMA

Ruth Chrisman

The Homestead Act allowed women, such as Ruth Chrisman and her sisters, to own their own land on the American prairie. These women rode horses and battled the elements, right alongside men.

0   400 miles
0   500 km

Glossary

blizzard heavy snowstorm, often with high winds. Animals and people sometimes get lost in a blizzard.

destiny events that are supposed to happen. Many people thought it was the destiny of the United States to stretch from the east coast to the west coast.

dugout kind of house that is dug out from the earth. A dugout home stays cool in summer and warm in winter.

Forty-Niner name given to the men and women who went to California in search of gold. They were called Forty-Niners because the Gold Rush started in 1849.

frontier unknown land, or the land beyond a border. In the mid-1800s, many Americans explored new frontiers.

herbal something made from plants. Medicines made from plant leaves, flowers, or roots are called herbal cures.

homestead land claimed by a settler. The Homestead Act of 1862 gave land to settlers who promised to live on it.

Mormon follower of the Church of Jesus Christ of Latter-Day Saints, a type of Christianity. This religion developed in the United States in the 1830s.

opportunity chance to get something better. U.S. pioneers in the 1800s looked for new opportunities out west.

pioneer settler who moves into an area where people do not live. In the United States, pioneers kept moving farther and farther west.

prairie land made up of open fields of grass. In the United States, states such as Kansas, Nebraska, and North and South Dakota are prairie states.

range open grasslands where cattle are raised. Before the settlers came, buffalo lived on the range.

reservation piece of land set aside for American Indians by the U.S. government. After the Indians were forced off their land in the 1800s, they were sent to live on reservations.

sawmill building where logs are cut into boards. Sawmills are an important part of the lumber business.

Sioux American Indian tribe, also called the Dakota. In the 1800s, the Sioux lived in western states such as Nebraska and Montana.

sod piece of earth held together by the roots of grass. Sod was used for roofs and burned for heat.

territory land claimed by a group or country. In the mid-1800s, land where Indians lived was known as Indian Territory. This land was eventually taken over by the U.S. government. During this same period, many areas in the west started out as territories, before later becoming official U.S. states.

treaty agreement between two sets of people. Nations often sign treaties after wars.

Find Out More

Books

Landau, Elaine. *The Homestead Act (A True Book)*. New York: Children's Press, 2006.

Warren, Andrea. *We Rode the Orphan Trains*. Boston: Houghton Mifflin, 2004.

Wilder, Laura Ingalls. *Little House in the Big Woods*. New York: HarperCollins, 2007 (first published 1932). (This is the first of the nine original "Little House" books.)

Websites

"National Orphan Train Complex"
www.orphantraindepot.com/index.html
Visit the website of the National Orphan Train Complex in Concordia, Kansas, to learn more about the experiences of many kids who were sent to the west.

"Gold Rush!"
pbskids.org/wayback/goldrush/index.html
This is a fun and interactive website full of information about the people and places of the Gold Rush.

Places to visit

Ingalls Homestead
20812 Homestead Road
De Smet, South Dakota 57231
www.ingallshomestead.com
Visit the Ingalls home, school, and other places of interest, which have all been restored by the Laura Ingalls Wilder Memorial Society.

Museum of the American West
4700 Western Heritage Way
Los Angeles, California 90027
theautry.org
This museum presents the history of the American West across many cultures. Special exhibits focus on the roles of women and American Indians.

Museum of the Westward Expansion
Jefferson National Expansion Memorial
Gateway Arch
11 North 4th Street
St. Louis, Missouri 63102
This museum covers all aspects of the westward expansion including the wagon trains of the later 1800s.

Index